THE

MEN

Gaby Wood is the author of a book on dolls which will be published by Faber in 1999. She is former deputy literary editor of the *Observer* and now works at the *London Review of Books*. She writes for the LRB, the *Observer*, the *Guardian*, and other publications.

THE SMALLEST OF
ALL PERSONS MENTIONED
IN THE RECORDS OF
LITTLENESS

GABY WOOD

P

PROFILE BOOKS
in association with
LONDON REVIEW OF BOOKS

First published
in book form in Great Britain in 1998 by
PROFILE BOOKS LTD
62 Queen Anne Street, London W1M 9LA

Previously published in 1997 by
LONDON REVIEW OF BOOKS
28 Little Russell Street, London WC1A 2HN

Photo credits: pages 9, 11, 12, 37, 41, 49, 51, The Royal College
of Surgeons of England; page 15, The British Library; page 29,
the Yale Centre for British Art, Paul Mellon Collection
Author photo by Jan Coghlan

Typeset in Quadraat
Designed by Peter Campbell
Printed and bound in Great Britain by
St Edmundsbury Press, Bury St Edmunds

A CIP catalogue record for this book is available
from the British Library.
ISBN 1 86197 088 9

THE SMALLEST OF ALL PERSONS
MENTIONED IN THE RECORDS
OF LITTLENESS

In memory of Maurice Hatton

IN THE CENTRE of the room there are two skeletons. Charles Byrne, the Irish Giant, faces the front. His skeleton, tainted brown because of the speed and secrecy of its preparation, is seven feet ten inches tall. So towering are the bones, and so impossibly hefty is their accompanying leather boot, that it's easy to walk past without noticing the adjacent filigree form. Mounted at eye-level, with its back to you as you look at the giant, is the skeleton of Caroline Crachami: tiny, clean, almost transparent. It stands with the support of a metal rod, which is threaded along the spine and pokes out from the skull. The vertebrae could be beads in a large necklace, the ribs starched lace, the fingers fallen milk teeth. The height given for the whole is one foot ten and a half inches. The smallness and the proportion of the thing (an adult shape the size of a newborn) are breathtaking, and from the back it is possible to see the articulated ivories (the marionette shoulders, the butterfly hips) as a work of art, a windless mobile. But the view from the front makes its one-time personhood inescapable: bottomless eye-sockets, a dark triangle for a nose, a pointless smile.

Caroline Crachami was once Britain's most famous dwarf. There was some confusion about what happened to the body after her early death: it had been sold, or stolen; there were conflicting accounts. What is certain is that Caroline Crachami died in 1824, and that her skeleton is now on display in the Hunterian Museum in London. Cabinets full of specimens line the walls; each jar is labelled with a letter and a number. I walk past an opossum's prehensile toes, a monkey's foot, a cross-section of a camel's hoof, a horse's shin. On the higher shelves are smaller things – bats and frogs and sea-horses; a fledgling toucanet.

The Hunterian is part of the Royal College of Surgeons. It is sometimes used for teaching, and is open to the public. John Hunter (1728-93), said by some to be the first person to articulate an ele-

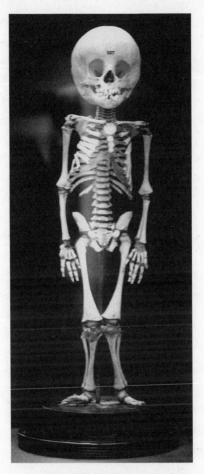

A pointless smile: the skeleton in the cabinet

phant's skeleton, was the younger brother of William Hunter. Both men were pioneering teachers of anatomy. The museum was set up to house John's anatomical collection, which has been called his 'great unwritten book'. Other such collections were either mere taxonomies or else forms of entertainment – ghoulish side-shows. Hunter's idea was to categorise the specimens so that they would speak for themselves, and explain the way he thought nature worked. His Physiological Series was designed to show the interrelation of structure and function in living things – plant, animal or human. The exhibition cases are divided not according to species but according to actions: walking and running, or digestion. Hence the opossum's toes next to a gorilla's hand, or a boar's jaw next to the dental pulp of an Indian elephant. Hunter's exhibits worked up from the most simple examples to the most complex, so that even those who were just beginning to study anatomy or physiology could understand. When he died, the collection comprised 13,682 specimens.

The Hunterian circa 1860. Watercolour sketch by T.H. Shepherd

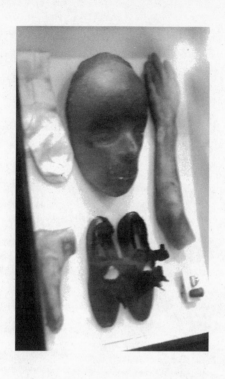

The clinical shrine: Crachami's relics on display

In his spare time, Hunter was a collector of other things. The objects he gathered as curios and those he needed for his research overlapped, as did the anatomical lessons and the sideshows. One of Hunter's biographers, John Kobler, claims that he owned a portrait of Caroline Crachami among his paintings of freaks. Though the painting is in the Hunterian collection, it can't have belonged to Hunter, since he died before Crachami was born. He can't, therefore, have known about the skeleton either, but it is part of his curious legacy that the girl's body should have been brought here.

Below the skeleton, near the floor, is another exhibit: a small, glass-covered box containing a few Crachami relics – a pair of silk socks, grey ballerina slippers with black bows and the inscription of the shoemaker on the inside, a thimble, a ruby ring. They might all have belonged to a doll. In among the possessions, as if they were the same kind of remnant, are wax casts of their owner: the foot the shoes used to fit, the arm whose fingers wore the ring and thimble, a death mask. It's an odd mix, a kind of clinical shrine. The prime purpose of the wax and the skeleton must be to prove that the small human existed; that someone at this institution once held her in his hands, made casts of her body, and articulated her skeleton. They may be intended as evidence, but they look more like trophies; either way, they are invitations to work backwards, to find out what the child's life was, and how, in death, she came to be here.

¶

SHE WAS EXHIBITED as Miss Crachami, the Sicilian Fairy, or Sicilian Dwarf. Not much is known about her; what there is comes from a pamphlet written to accompany the original exhibition, three reports in the *Times*, a number of contemporary allusions, and several articles written for medical journals in a subsequent attempt to figure out her condition. In 1978, Richard Altick put together the pieces of her story in *The Shows of London*. Until very recently (as far as I could tell), Altick was the only person outside the medical

A

BRIEF MEMOIR

OF

MISS CRACHAMI

THE CELEBRATED

Sicilian Dwarf;

WITH

SKETCHES

OF

SONOPAS, BEBE, BORULAWSKI, SIR JEFFERY
HUDSON,

AND OTHER DIMINUTIVE PERSONS.

———————

London:

PRINTED BY W. T. MONCRIEFF,

Drury Lane Printing Office,

104, Drury Lane, corner of Clare Court.

FOR THE PROPRIETOR; AND SOLD AT THE EXHIBITION, 22, NEW
BOND STREET.

1824.

The cover of Crachami's exhibition pamphlet of 1824

profession who had written about her this century. Now Jan Bondeson, whose paper on her appeared in the *American Journal of Medical Genetics* in 1992, has published a book aimed at a wider audience, called *A Cabinet of Medical Curiosities*, which includes, among chapters on spontaneous human combustion and maternal impressions, a section about Crachami, a lightly rewritten version of his earlier article.

More curiously, Christine Borland, one of the artists shortlisted for the Turner Prize 1997, had as one part of her exhibition at the Tate Gallery an installation devoted to the Sicilian Dwarf and the Irish Giant. The installation is called *After a True Story – Giant and Fairy Tales*, and is made up of four pieces, one on each wall. There are two plates of glass, positioned like shelves, and two books, held open at the same page. The smaller piece of glass, which is placed low down on its wall, is covered with an impression in dust of Crachami's skeleton. It is a delicate stencil, made as one might decorate a cake with icing sugar. A light shines onto the glass so the shadow of the dust-shape falls on the wall. The giant is stencilled on a larger pane, placed high up on the other wall. Each body throws a soft white, barely visible double image of itself at the viewer, a shade of a shade. The leather-bound books are two copies of something called *Giant and Fairy Tales* (they look like antiquarian relics, though I can't find a record of the book's publication). Crachami's life story is on the left-hand page, the giant's on the right. Both are said to be adapted from the display panel at the Hunterian Museum. It is difficult to know whether the glass and the dust, beautiful and haunting though they are, would work without the stories in the book. They are made to work together, but the point of the piece, and the force of it, seem to come mainly from the words.

The current convergence of interest in these remains must say something about the kinds of stories we are ready to hear. Or about anatomy or memory – our relationship to our insides or our relationship to the dead.

In the weeks before she died, Crachami had been exhibited at 22 New Bond Street in London.

This was 20 years before Phineas Taylor Barnum arrived from America with Tom Thumb. The *Times* declared Crachami 'unquestionably the most curious of all the dwarfish candidates for public favour that have visited this metropolis'. The 'Brief Memoir' in the 1824 exhibition pamphlet claims her as 'the smallest of all persons mentioned in the records of littleness'.

She was born in Palermo, or so the story goes, the day after the Battle of Waterloo, making her nine years minus 15 days when she died. Her penniless Sicilian parents were said to have moved to Ireland, where her father was hired as a musician by the Theatre Royal in Dublin. But Caroline was consumptive, and when a Dr Gilligan, who showed a peculiar interest in the child, told them that the climate in England would be better for her health, the parents allowed her to go with him. They agreed that Gilligan would exhibit their daughter for a short period of time once they reached London, since he insisted that, 'as a man of science, he was anxious that such an extraordinary phenomenon should not be lost to the physiological world.'

Crachami was exhibited in Liverpool, Birmingham and Oxford before reaching her fashionable exhibition room in Mayfair. She was quite a hit. The *Morning Chronicle* began its report: 'There are some persons who emerge from obscurity of a sudden, and from being known by nobody, become the leading topic of conversation and the centre of a brilliant circle.' Within a few weeks that brilliant circle was said to include 'different branches of the Royal Family', 'more than three hundred of the nobility' and 'nearly three thousand distinguished fashionables'. On 12 April, she was received at Carlton House by King George IV, who, it was reported, 'expressed great pleasure at her appearance'. So many people came to see Crachami that she was soon exhausted. In fact, she might have died of exhaustion, had TB not got her first. On Thursday, 3 June, she received more than two hundred visitors. That evening (according to the *Times*) 'a languor appeared to come over her, and on her way from the exhibition-room she expired.'

The accounts of those who saw Crachami have the sort of smiling condescension about them one might expect to be directed at a public curiosity, or even, more ordinarily, at a young girl. Crachami was not a horror attraction, like her more famous successor, the Elephant Man (whom his rescuer Frederick Treves described, when he first found him in 1884, as 'the most disgusting specimen of humanity that I have ever seen'). The general sense of wonder surrounding the Sicilian Fairy was to do with her being an adult in miniature, or with her resemblance to a doll. Leslie Fiedler, in *Freaks: Myths and Images of the Secret Self* (1978), identified what he called 'scale freaks' as the most enduring; Crachami's main strength as an exhibit was certainly her ability to befuddle her viewers' sense of scale. (A decade or so later, Dickens wrote about a dwarf exhibited at Greenwich Fair who arrived in a box 'painted outside like a six-roomed house'. The crowd, seeing him fire a pistol from the first-floor window, 'verily believe that it is his ordinary town residence, divided like other mansions into drawing rooms, dining parlour, and bedchambers'.) 'It is impossible to describe the miracle of her appearance, or its effect upon the mind,' the *Literary Gazette* wrote of Crachami. 'To see . . . all the faculties of humanity in a being so inconceivably below the standard at which we have ever witnessed them, so overturns all previous impressions, that, even with the fact before us, we doubt the evidence of our own senses. A tolerable sized doll, acting and speaking, would not astonish us so much.'

Crachami's fairy-like qualities made her all the more easy to appropriate; she became the pet of each person who passed by the exhibition, and a sign announced that she could be 'handled' by anyone who was willing to pay an extra shilling. There was clearly some element of fantasy involved in watching her, and, I find, a murky flirtatiousness of tone in much of the writing about her. The viewer's imaginings are what come across most strongly, and what we might be able to tell about her person is clouded.

The fantasies surrounding Crachami begin

with the story of her birth. Sir Everard Home (a surgeon who was to have a starring role in Crachami's afterlife) reports this reason for her dwarfism. Crachami's mother was three months pregnant, and travelling on the Continent in the baggage caravan of the Duke of Wellington's army. (Home doesn't explain how she came to be there.) There was a violent storm in the middle of the night, and a monkey, which had been chained to the roof, found its way inside. To keep itself warm, the monkey got between her legs. 'Half-asleep', Home writes, the woman 'put her hand down to scratch herself, but scratching the monkey it bit her fingers, and threw her into fits'. When the baby was born six months later, it weighed one pound, and measured seven inches.

Home was a believer in the teratologist idea that 'maternal impressions' were a cause of freaks. What was meant by 'impression' was a psychological imprinting – a sort of physical manifestation of the unconscious. In one of Home's examples, a woman is robbed on a dark evening by an artilleryman with a hare lip. She gives birth to a child with a hare lip. The baby, like a dream, is born of fear. The introduction of the monkey in the Crachami story can be accounted for by working backwards from her looks. One writer commented that 'there is a little of the simia in her features'. But that the monkey should have been between the mother's legs, and that she should only have noticed it when she reached down to 'scratch herself', looks like a projection of another kind.

There are different registers of fantasy where reports on Crachami are concerned, some more fraught or covert or lighthearted than others, but they are all part of the same overdetermined world.

Someone who at that time wrote a column in the *Literary Gazette and Journal* called 'Sights of London, etc' (and whom Richard Altick believes may have been the editor, William Jerdan) described her as 'the fairy of your superstition in actual life'. One memoirist wrote of William Jerdan's life that 'if its historian cannot describe it as altogether creditable, it was certainly useful'. The

Literary Gazette, and Jerdan in particular, was renowned for fostering the talent of a young and unprecedentedly popular poet. Letitia Landon, who wrote under the initials LEL, published her first poem in the journal when she was fifteen, and her first book appeared the year Crachami was exhibited. Landon's life was crushed by scandal, and she died in 1838 in mysterious circumstances. Jerdan was not involved in the mystery, or even in the final circumstances, but descriptions of Landon as a child-woman show how the categories of age and maturity could be elided into something more peculiar, how some of the qualities Jerdan and others saw in Landon might be akin to those popularly seen in Crachami. Samuel Carter Hall's wife found LEL, on first meeting, 'a bright-eyed, sparkling, restless little girl ... frolicking from subject to subject with the playfulness of a spoiled child. ... [P]ositively as she grew older [she] looked younger – her delicate complexion, the transparent tenderness of her skin, and the playful expression of her child-like features adding to the deception'. Jerdan remembered her as 'a plump girl, grown enough to be almost mistaken for a woman', bowling a hoop with one hand and holding a book in the other.

Jerdan devoted a good deal of space in the *Literary Gazette* to Crachami over a number of weeks, but always as if he was sharing a joke with the reader. On his first visit, Jerdan picked up Crachami, 'caressed, and saluted her; and it was most laughable to see her resent the latter freedom, wiping her cheek, and expressing her dislike of the rough chin'. In his next column, he implies an impossible romance between himself and the child: 'I am sure my readers will be very glad to hear that I have accommodated matters with my fair friend, Miss Crachami. Feeling for the mortification under which I must be labouring, in consequence of her jilting me, she had even the condescension to visit me in person . . . I can only say I can say no more.' As a service to his readers, he measures the girl himself, and reports that her 'real height' is 19 inches and a half, the length of her foot three inches and one-eighth, the length of her fore-finger ('she would not give me the wedding one') one inch and seven-eighths, and so on.

The comedian Charles Mathews's visit comes to us via the filter of his wife, who wrote his memoirs. There is an element of sexual jealousy in her tone:

The lady was a most disgusting little withered creature (although young), very white, and, what my husband disliked very much in any woman, had a *powdery* look upon her skin. Her voice was pitched in the highest key of childish treble, indeed so thin, and comb-like, that it hardly reached the ear of those to whom she spoke.

Mathews guessed that Gilligan, who called himself the child's father, was not Italian, as he claimed to be. He

startled the foreigner . . . by asking significantly, whether it was Palermo in the county of Cork where he was born? at this inquiry, the man leered at him in an arch manner, scratching his head for a moment, and rubbing his cheek with his hand, as if puzzled how to treat the question. At last, he winked his eye, and putting his finger to the side of his nose, said, 'Och! I see your honour's a deep 'un! Sure, you're right, but don't peach!'

Gilligan tried to keep him quiet by saying he could 'handle Miss Crackham' (as Mrs Mathews calls her) for free. But Mathews, his wife reports, 'had forebearance enough to decline this liberality and the opportunity proffered'.

When it came to announcing Crachami's death, William Jerdan wrote that the frequency of the *Literary Gazette*'s 'mention of this extraordinary Being, may have shown that we felt a kindly interest in her welfare', but Crachami's admirers seem to have been blind to the implications of some of the things they themselves reported. 'Yet the great wonder,' Jerdan went on to say, as if her welfare were subordinate to the wonder, 'was that the machinery of life could have been carried on for so long in so minute and diminutive a form.' (The exhibition pamphlet, on the other hand, had boasted that there was 'every probability of her living to a considerable age'.) Clearly Crachami's physical condition was appalling. Everyone who saw her noticed what Jerdan calls her 'strange, unearthly voice', and her walk was said to be 'very tottering'. We are told she was 'prodigious' because attracted to bright objects, and that she liked to tap her foot in time to music – is it possible that she was simply a very small child? If given biscuits she would say, 'Good, good,' and pat her stomach. Pointing to her ear-rings she would exclaim: 'Very pretty.' Jerdan, impressed, tells us that 'she has already learnt a little English'. But did anyone try speaking to her in Italian? It seems more likely that these few words of English were her first in any language.

The most eloquent invocation of the seedy setup was made by the poet Thomas Hood, who used Crachami's exhibition to illustrate the price of fame, or of visibility, even in a person who was hardly visible to begin with. (Hood may have had in mind a sketch by John Augustus Atkinson which shows a man standing in the doorway of a darkened caravan, pointing to a large board which advertises 'THE SICILIAN FAIRY ONLY 2&6'. A crowd has gathered outside.) The poem is Hood's 'Ode to The Great Unknown', addressed to Sir Walter Scott. Why, Hood wonders, is Scott never to be seen, though his works are so widely

The Show:
*Crachami on the
road. Lithograph
by John Augustus
Atkinson*

read ('Parent of many children – child of none!')? At the end of nine intricately rhymed pages, Hood lightheartedly concludes that there must be something physically wrong with Scott ('Why, but because thou art some puny Dwarf'). Well, Hood decides, Scott is right to shy away from the public,

For certainly the first pernicious man
That ever saw thee, would quickly draw thee
In some vile literary caravan
    Shown for a shilling
    Would be thy killing,
Think of Crachami's miserable span!
No tinier frame the tiny spark could dwell in
    Than there it fell in –
But when she felt herself a show, she tried
To shrink from the world's eye, poor dwarf! and died!'

¶

I STOP ON my way home to buy some fish for dinner. Across the road from the fishmongers is a shop I have been curious about for some time. Roaring wild cats and scattered ornithology are on display in the window. There is always a secure metal grill over the front and a sign on the door explaining that all the animals inside died of natural causes. Until now, I had never seen the shop open.

As I enter, two old ladies are on their way out. They stare at my plastic bag.

'Oh,' I say, 'it's fish.' They seem to expect more of a story. 'I mean it's fresh fish. I'm going to eat it.'

They wrinkle their noses at this explanation and giggle as they walk out of the door, waving towards the back of the shop. I stand at the entrance for a moment, taking in the bats and birds hanging from the ceiling, the lions and tigers and bears, the miscellaneous antlers on the walls, the toucan, the sharks' teeth, the rabbit. I make my way forwards, skirting various household pets (these are more unsettling than the rest; as a reflex, my hand reaches out to stroke some tabby or labrador, and has to pull back from a glassy-eyed greeting). At the far end, beside a man at a desk, are jars of stuff, not taxidermy, but pickled things – anatomical contraband.

'What's this?' I ask, pointing to a container of

floating pink.

'That,' announces the man, in the tone grown-ups use to give children the spooks, 'is a human foetus.'

'A real one?'

'Yes. A Real Human Foetus.'

'I see,' I say. 'Have you been to the Hunterian Museum?'

'Nooo,' says the man, as if for the millionth time. 'Not yet. They've got things in jars there, have they?'

'Yeh. And they've also got a midget skeleton.' He raises an eyebrow.

'Ah,' he gloats, 'but is it really a midget skeleton? I mean, we get them in all the time, saying they're midget skeletons. They say that, but they're really just baby skeletons. For instance, look over there, now what would you say that was?' He's pointing to something behind me.

'I'd say that was a newborn baby skeleton.'

'Oh. Yeh. It is.'

Despite his disappointment, the man doesn't miss a beat: 'There's a legend about a midget skeleton, isn't there? I saw it on Fortean TV. Something about a sailor who got smaller and smaller and when his coffin had to be made it was tiny. And ever since then there's been a curse on anyone who's had the coffin in their possession. Probably why people keep trying to pass their baby skeletons off as midgets.'

On my next visit to the Hunterian, I thought about the taxidermist, and the people who were trying to flog him babies' bones. His question was more pertinent than I had realised. Was Crachami really a midget? In the museum, to the side of the skeletons' cabinet, there is a display panel headed 'Caroline Crachami: A Cranio-Dental Study'. Apparently, the first time anyone had thought to look at her teeth was quite late, in the 1950s. But it was only in the past year or so that her dentition was compared with that of contemporary children of known age. In the x-rays from the Fifties, Crachami's teeth had been shown to be comparable to those of a child aged between two and three, though the height of the skeleton was that of a newborn. Either she had a condition which retarded her dentition along with the rest of her body (which previous work on dwarfism showed to be unlikely) or she was not, as had been claimed, nine years old. This would not have been the first time a midget was said, for publicity purposes, to have been older than she (or he) was, but such a wide discrepancy was surprising. The authors of the new 'cranio-dental study' had investigated the entire dentition: they had made their new comparisons, they had drawn new graphs and taken new x-rays. They found what her attraction to bright objects and shrill, stilted speech had already implied: Caroline Crachami was actually three.

As far as my unscientist's mind can follow, the first diagnosis of her condition was made by Sir Hastings Gilford in 1902, when her age was still taken to be nine. His theory was that she suffered from a form of overall growth retardation which could not be accounted for by any of the known causes of dwarfism, something he chose to call 'ateleiosis' ('not arriving at perfection'). In 1960, after the first set of x-rays, H.P.G. Seckel described a form of 'bird-headed dwarfism', which is now called Seckel syndrome, and claimed Crachami had suffered from it. The most striking symptom of bird-headed dwarfism is, as you would expect, the one from which it derives its name. But Crachami's death mask shows no signs of the beaked nose and receding chin Seckel supposed she had. It is possible that he based his theory, as Gilford had done, on a portrait of Crachami in the Hunterian collection. This is the painting John Kobler claims was bought by John Hunter. In fact, it was presented to the College in 1827 by Sir Everard Home. The portrait shows a profile and a full-face view of a shrunken, monkey-like invalid dressed in a black dress with a white ruff. It was painted – from memory – by Alfred Edward Chalon, RA (1781-1860), and when it came into the College's possession, it was said to be 'very little like' her. Chalon was widely patronised by the aristocracy, and later received the title of 'Portrait-painter in water-colours to Her Majesty', but he was also known for his ferocious caricatures. It is perhaps no accident that in his portrait Crachami bears a stronger resemblance to some of his cartoon characters than she does to his flattered ladies.

Dr. F. Majewski, writing in the *American Journal of Medical Genetics* in 1992, in response to Jan Bondeson's historical sketch in that publication, proposed that Crachami may have suffered from a new type of dwarfism, one of the main symptoms of which is severe intrauterine growth-retardation. He compared her case to that of two siblings born in the 1970s and 80s. Amongst other things, they had, like Crachami, very high-pitched voices, and their profiles (as seen in photographs accompanying the article) are strikingly, even movingly, similar. They have pointed but not beaked noses, and steep foreheads. Majewski discounted Seckel syndrome and termed this new group 'osteodysplastic primordial dwarfism type III'. Bondeson thought Crachami did not quite fit into Majewski's category. Less than two years ago the same journal published an article written by six Italian paediatricians (Boscherini et al.), who claimed to have exam-

Portrait of Crachami by Alfred Edward Chalon,
presented to the College in 1827

ined a patient so similar to Crachami that another new type could be identified. They called it, 'in tribute', Type Caroline Crachami. Their patient was 'extroverted and sociable but mildly mentally retarded'. He had the same facial features, a high-pitched voice, and intrauterine growth retardation.

None of these verdicts has accepted the dental experts' opinion that Crachami was aged between two and three when she died. Jan Bondeson's view is that there is historical evidence that she was nine (I can only find reports possibly clouded by Gilligan's hype), and that a delay in the growth of teeth and bones is itself a feature of OPD (osteodysplastic primordial dwarfism), so does not contradict any of the paediatricians' theses.

This is not a debate I can join, or even properly understand. But I would like to find out what you could see, if you knew about these things, in the skeleton itself. Clearly the height is wrong for a three-year-old (and certainly for a nine-year-old), but the proportions seem so regular that I wonder what could be told about the skeleton at a glance, or, say, from a photograph.

A friend refers me to the person she calls the Bone Man. I arrive at the fusty institution where he works armed with a slightly blurred photo I have taken of Crachami's skeleton, and as I pull it out I realise how unfair it is to ask him to judge on such poor evidence. But I only need a general idea. The Bone Man looks surprisingly young. I don't know what I'd imagined, a career in some temporal proportion to the bones studied, perhaps. But he must be in his thirties; he has scruffy reddish hair, a short beard and glasses. His accent has a Cockney edge to it, and he says the word 'bones' ('bah-oons') with more relish than I have previously encountered. He takes the photo; his eyes scan it slowly from top to bottom; his brow furrows.

In all his experience, the Bone Man says, he has never seen anything like it. He's seen achondroplastic dwarfs, where the limbs are very short, but never anything like this. He says it must be very rare.

I ask him whether the skeleton is really as well proportioned as it seems to me.

'Well, the tibias look slightly short, but that depends on the child. Really, for a two-year-old the skull should be bigger in relation to the body. But the proportions are surprisingly regular.'

'And what about that slight forward curvature of the spine?'

'A certain amount of curvature wouldn't be abnormal. It all depends on how the skeleton's been assembled and how they've hung it.' He peers at the blur. 'It's very hard to tell.'

The process of articulating the bones was another thing that interested me. I kept thinking about the moment in *Our Mutual Friend* when Mr Venus, 'Preserver of Animals and Birds, Articulator of human bones', shouts a threat to a boy who has unintentionally taken a stray molar with his three-pence change: 'Don't sauce me, in the wicious pride of your youth; . . . you've no idea how small you'd come out, if I had the articulating of you.' Who had the articulating of Crachami's small frame? Whose idea was it to make the

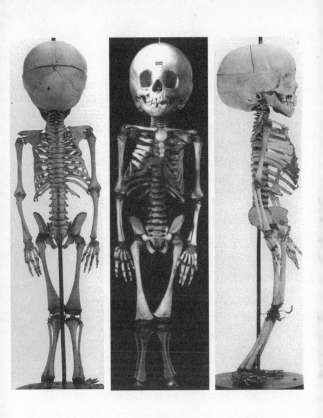

Crachami's skeleton, front, back and side.

wax casts?

William Clift, first conservator of the Hunterian, is usually referred to as Hunter's 'devoted amanuensis' and sometimes simply as 'poor Clift'. He had been an apprentice to Hunter since his 17th birthday, and is said to have had a particular flair for drawing and calligraphy. It fell to him to dissect Crachami's body, and to prepare the skeleton. But its arrival at the College was due to Sir Everard Home, who was at that time President of the Royal College of Surgeons and Sergeant-Surgeon to the King. The Donations Book of the Hunterian Museum for 1824 records that on 7 June, 'the body of Miss or Mademoiselle Crachami, the Sicilian dwarf' was brought by Sir E. Home, 'in a box'. In the *Lectures on Comparative Anatomy* in which Home mentions Crachami, he offers no explanation for how he came by her remains. He merely writes: 'I saw it several times while alive, and it came into my possession after death.'

¶

CRACHAMI's death, and the story surrounding it, were reported in the *Times*. But many questions were left unasked. If she was only three, how could her parents have let her go? Were they in fact her parents, or had they snatched her from a freak show themselves? Did money change hands when Gilligan took her away? There is no evidence other than the newspaper story, and the drama that follows requires a belief in the parents' distress.

On Monday, 14 June 1824, a man named Lewis Fogle appeared at Marlborough Street magistrate's office and requested a warrant for Dr Gilligan's arrest. Fogle (also called Fogell Crachami in a later article in the *Times*) said he was the father of the child known as the Sicilian Dwarf. He had learnt of her death via the newspapers, and had come to claim the girl's body, so that her mother might have 'one look at her dear child before it was consigned to the earth'. The magistrate was unable to grant him the warrant, however, and he referred Fogle to the St James parish authorities, whose duty it was to see that an inquest was held on any person who had died suddenly. But the parish had no record of Crachami's death, and all Fogle's attempts to find Gilligan proved unsuccessful. On arrival at Gilligan's lodgings – the house of a Mr Dorlan in Duke Street – he was told that the Doctor had left the day after the child died, and that he'd taken her remains with him. Her tiny 'state-bed', and the outfit in which she had been presented to the King, were still there. Gilligan also left a debt of £25 to his landlord, whose own interest in Gilligan's whereabouts led him to help Fogle in his search. No one seemed to know where Gilligan was, or what he intended to do with Crachami's body – though Fogle's enquiries yielded one devastating possibility. Gilligan had been heard to say 'in the lifetime of the child, and while it was still being exhibited, that some members of the College of Surgeons had offered, if any misfortune should occur to cause the child's death, to give him £500 for the remains, for the purposes of dissection and the use of the College, to put amongst their collection of extraordinary instances of the whims and freaks of nature'.

This was the period which, as one historian put it, 'made body-snatching famous'. Another poem by Thomas Hood, a satirical ballad called 'Mary's Ghost', gives some idea of the possibilities and fears in play at the time. In the poem Mary's ghost visits her beloved William and says:

> The arm that used to take your arm
>   Is took to Dr. Vyse;
> And both my legs are gone to walk
>   the hospital at Guy's.
>
> I vowed that you should have my hand,
>   But Fate gives us denial;
> You'll find it there, at Doctor Bell's,
>   In spirits and a phial.
>
> As for my feet, the little feet
>   You used to call so pretty,
> There's one, I know in Bedford Row,
>   The t'other's in the city.
>
> I can't tell where my head is gone,
>   But Dr. Carpue can;
> As for my trunk, it's all packed up
>   To go by Pickford's van.

I wish you'd go to Mr. P
  And save me such a ride;
I don't half like the outside place
  They've took for my inside.

The cock it crows - I must be gone!
  My William, we must part!
But I'll be yours in death, although
  Sir Astley has my heart!

Don't go weep upon my grave,
  And think that there I be;
They haven't left an atom there
  Of my anatomie.

Until 1832, when the Anatomy Act was passed (making unclaimed paupers' corpses available to anatomists), the only legal supply of bodies for the anatomy schools was from the gallows. The death penalty formally involved not only hanging but also subsequent dissection. So when the dissectors made an offer for Crachami's body, it was an offer to treat her as only murderers were, legally, treated. (Jerdan remarked in one of his articles that Crachami's 'great antipathy is to Doctors; these have offended her by examining her too

46

minutely, and whenever they are mentioned she doubles her filbert of a fist, and manifests her decided displeasure').

By 1824 the resurrection men were, so to speak, in full swing. The practice was illegal but it was not secret, and public hostility rapidly increased. Some years earlier one of Hunter's students had written to his sister:

My room...in point of situation is not the most pleasant in the world. The Dissecting room with a half a dozen dead bodies in it is immediately above and that in which Mr. Hunter makes preparations is the next adjoining to it, so that you may conceive it to be a little perfumed. There is a dead carcase just at this moment rumbling up the stairs and the Resurrection Men swearing most terribly. I am informed this will be the case most mornings about four o'clock throughout the winter. There is something horrible in it at first but I am now become reconciled.

The going rate for a 'full-sized' body the year Crachami died is thought to have been around eight or nine guineas. Children – called 'large smalls' – cost less. 'Whims and freaks of nature', naturally, had no set price. There was, nevertheless, some precedent for the offer of £500. Charles Byrne, now the tower of bones that stands beside Crachami in the Hunterian Museum, was a famous giant, famously snatched. He was an alcoholic, he had TB; seeing that Byrne was soon to die, John Hunter made him an offer for his dead body. Byrne refused, and, horrified by the suggestion, ordered a lead coffin to be made. He asked the undertaker to have a team of corpse-watchers on hand for when his time came, and said that his coffin should be thrown into the sea before Hunter or his colleagues could lay their hands on him. Undeterred, Hunter hired his own man to keep an eye on Byrne. His man eventually found the corpse-watchers in the pub across the way, and the £500 price was arrived at over a few drinks. As soon as Hunter got hold of the body, he prepared the skeleton and then kept it hidden for two years. Then, having thus far escaped attention, he put Byrne's bones on display.

It is not known who made the offer for Crachami's body. Byrne's was such a famous story that Gilligan might have made his up. In any case, her

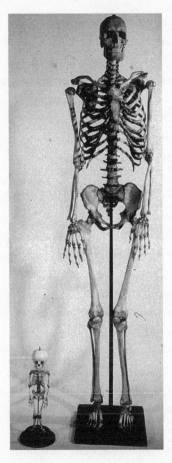

The Sicilian
Dwarf and
the Irish
Giant

body was not taken to the College directly. When Fogle heard about the offer he retraced Gilligan's steps, visiting first the private establishment of Joshua Brookes, a talented teacher of practical anatomy who was excluded from the College of Surgeons because he was not 'a gentleman'. (One contemporary described Brookes as 'without exception the dirtiest professional person I have ever met with . . . I really know no dirty thing with which he could compare – all and every part of him was dirt.') Brookes told Fogle that Gilligan had indeed come to him, and that he'd asked for 100 guineas in exchange for the dwarf. Brookes had refused. Fogle went to the other private anatomy schools; none held Crachami's body. Next he went to the public hospitals, where, the *Times* reported, he 'was shown all the subjects, but could not identify his tiny offspring'. In despair, he returned to Duke Street, where Dorlan 'from some circumstances' advised him to visit Sir Everard Home in Sackville Street. Fogle was met at the door by Home himself. 'Oh,' said Home, 'you have come from Gilligan about the

Thomas Rowlandson's satire: said to be William Hunter's dissecting room, the drawing is clearly also a more general comment on the times.

dwarf. The surgeons have not yet held a meeting, therefore I can't say what sum will be voted to him.'

Gilligan, evidently, had come to Sackville Street the week before, 'with the body of the child, and expressed a wish to dispose of it'. He and Home were already acquainted: Home, as we know, had visited the exhibition several times, and it was through Home's influence that Crachami had been presented at Court. Home had apparently refused to buy the girl's remains, but said he would pass the body on to the College of Surgeons, who would decide how much they wanted to pay. Gilligan accepted the arrangement, but said he was leaving town, and would send a messenger to pick up the money. When Fogle appeared at the door and mentioned his daughter, Home assumed he was Gilligan's envoy. Fogle burst into tears and begged to be allowed one last look at his 'beloved infant'. Home gave him a note which would grant him entry to the College, and a personal cheque for ten pounds, promising, as gentlemen do, to 'represent the unfortunate business to His Majesty'.

Fogle sped along to Surgeons' Hall, 'in a state bordering on insanity' according to the *Times*, hoping to prevent the anatomisation of the child. He was more than a week too late. He was shown into a room where 'the first thing that caught his view' was said to be 'the body of his darling progeny'. Fogle fell upon his daughter's remains and could not be prised away, until the surgeons promised nothing further would be done to the body. He left for Ireland immediately, to 'communicate the dreadful intelligence to his wife'.

¶

THE CURATOR of the Hunterian tells me what a resource the Royal College of Surgeons' museums are. They have specimens taken from people who died of syphilis and smallpox – things we can now cure. It's important for students who will be dealing with these diseases to see what would happen if they were left untreated. The crucial thing about the skeletons is that people are still learning from them. They're not just curiosities: 'An American orthopaedic specialist who came here some years ago was very interested in the base of the spine of the Irish giant,' she tells me. 'He said it was a perfect illustration of something he had been trying to demonstrate to his students. We made a slide for him.' She, too, says that the case on Crachami's condition is far from closed. 'I hope that one day someone may come along and say that this is X . . .'

As we talk, the heroes and villains of the institution – Hunter and Home and Clift – are spoken about almost as if they were alive. We discuss who might have offered Gilligan money, what part Home might have had in the saga. (In the year before Crachami died, Home fell drastically out of favour. He had plagiarised Hunter's unpublished manuscripts – he was Hunter's executor – and then burned them all so that he wouldn't be found out.) So much, she says, is conjecture.

I ask what exactly is involved in the preparation of a skeleton.

'The organs and flesh would be removed and then, in order to eliminate all traces of flesh and fat, the body would be boiled down.'

'Would records have been kept?'

'Not for something as straightforward as that.'

Later on, rereading one of the articles on Crachami, I notice a reference to William Clift's 'manuscript account of his findings'. I call the curator.

'Well, the building was bombed in 1941. Many of the records were lost.'

'But if they hadn't been lost, where would they be?'

'They would be in the library here.'

The room is beautiful: huge windows, heavy oak tables, a gallery of bookshelves, and one or two display cases containing some of Hunter's dissection tools. On a desk is William Clift's diary, a hefty tome, marbled in grey and yellow and orange, with a brown leather spine and corners. On a rectangle of brown paper is written 'Richards's Universal Daily Remembrancer 1824 Enlarged edition, Price 6s'.

Clift's artistic lettering fills the pages: a tiny,

slanted, perfectly uniform script, the brown ink heavier at the start of each line, the insertions and crossings-out as neat as the rest. His dissection notes on 'Miss Crachami' are dated 8 and 9 June. The unfamiliar terms float up to my eyes: 'The stomach and intestinal canal very large for so small a creature', 'the uterus extremely minute, as well as the Ovaria', 'the lungs almost entirely covered with whitish irregular spots, and very much tuberculated throughout its substance', 'very small fontanelle still remaining unossified'.

At the top of the page, next to the name and the date, there is a special note. One thing stands out from the rest: 'The labia pudenda Nymphae and Anus in a state of putrefaction on Monday – shewing that they had been in a high state of irritation'. Lower down, Clift offers an explanation: a blister on the chest had 'probably' caused the bladder to become distended, and urine to be passed with difficulty. Maybe so, but why then the special note? And if this element of the autopsy was important enough to warrant a separate mention, why have none of the articles which make use of other aspects of the examination quoted it? It would seen relevant, perhaps, to the intrauterine growth retardation which is symptomatic of osteodysplastic primordial dwarfism, or at least to the likely urinary tract infections attendant upon it. Jan Bondeson quotes the autopsy report in full in a 'Further Note' published in the *American Journal of Medical Genetics* a year after his original article, but he omits this detail. In his new book, he specifically says after commenting on the distended bladder that 'no further examination of these parts was undertaken.' His phrase seems to be answering an unasked question, though he may be paraphrasing Everard Home, who, Bondeson goes on say, 'concluded that the monkey's grip on the loins of the mother had caused this affliction of the bladder when the child was in utero'. From the Greeks to the Victorians, maternal impressions were used to explain anomalous births, but in this case the mother seems a long way off, and one might venture to think that Crachami's visitors made even more of an impression on her than she did on them.

I am not the first person to have told this story. One of the features of Crachami's life is that she left few traces, and that anyone who wants to follow it will find the same clues. But there is always, I think, room for rereadings, for new configurations and for reflections in a different light. My first and best guide was Richard Altick, in his *The Shows of London* (1978). Those who wish to be led further back will find the main components of the case in Crachami's exhibition pamphlet, *Memoirs of Miss Crachami, the celebrated Sicilian Dwarf* (1824); in Edward J Wood's *Giants and Dwarfs* (1868); in the *Memoirs of Charles Mathews*, Vol IV, by Mrs Mathews (1839); in the *Times* of 1824, on 10, 15 and 17 June; the *Morning Chronicle* of that same year, 17 April, and 8 and 13 May; in the *Literary Gazette*, again 1824, on 17 April, 15 May, and 12 and 19 June.

I have made use of a number of articles relating to her medical condition, most of which are referred to in the text. I could add Jessie Dobson's

– 'The Story of Caroline Crachami' in the *Annals of the Royal College of Surgeons* (1955), and a more precise reference for Everard Home's *Lectures on Comparative Anatomy*: Vol. V (1828). Theya Molleson and Margaret Cox's fascinating work on the *Spitalfields Project* (Vol. II, 1993), though I haven't gone into it here, has some bearing on the anthropology of Crachami's skeleton.

In my circlings around the subject I have been helped by biographies and books about John Hunter (which are also concerned with William Hunter, Everard Home, William Clift; their times and their peers): notably Jessie Dobson's (1969), John Kobler's (1960), Jane Marion Oppenheimer's (1964), and George Qvist's (1981) and Home's biographical preface to Hunter's *Treatise on the blood, inflammation and gun-shot wounds* (1796).

On the subject of bodysnatching, Ruth Richardson's *Death, Dissection and the Destitute* (1987) is engrossing and incomparable. Roger French's essay on 'The Anatomical Tradition' in the *Routledge Companion Encyclopaedia of the History of Medi-*

cine (eds W F Bynum and Roy Porter, Vol I 1993) is a useful addition, and Martin Fido's popular (if at times unreliable) *Bodysnatchers* (1988) is a lively one.

The cameo parts of William Jerdan and LEL, Thomas Hood, Alfred Chalon, and the Elephant Man were researched with the principal aid of Jerdan's *Autobiography* (1852) and Samuel Carter Hall's *A Book of Memories of Great Men and Women of the age, from personal acquaintance* (1870); Thomas Hood's *Odes and Addresses* (1825), and his *Whims and Oddities* (1826); an exhibition catalogue of Chalon's work at the Musée Rath in Geneva (1971); Frederick Treves's *The Elephant Man and Other Reminiscences* (1923) and Ashley Montagu's *The Elephant Man* (1971).

For a general background on freaks, monsters, and theories relating to them, I read, with most interest, Aristotle's *Generation of Animals* (Loeb edition, trans. A L Peck, 1943), Ambroise Paré's *Des monstres et prodiges* (1573, critical edition 1971), and Leslie Fiedler's (now seminal) *Freaks: Myths and Images of the Secret Self* (1978). The Memoirs of an earlier famous dwarf, Joseph Boruwlaski (1788) are well worth digging up; and a novel, Walter de la Mare's wonderful *Memoirs of a Midget* (1921), gives a different tint to the tale.

Another novelist has haunted this project. Although I have only made specific reference to *Our Mutual Friend* and a section of *Sketches by Boz*, the ghost of Charles Dickens roams free. London is a sneaking, nook-and-cranny monument to the characters who shared or wrote about Crachami's world. There is still so much left of those times, and perhaps the best, most insistent sources are this city's streets.

London, March 1998.

THANKS are due (in some cases overdue) to Mary-Kay Wilmers, Nicholas Spice, and all at the *London Review of Books*. To the Curator and Librarians at the Hunterian; the Bone Man; the Taxidermist. To Dr. Caroline Grigson, Isobel Armstrong, Jo McDonagh, Vicky Peters and Michael Wood.

'The Smallest of all Persons Mentioned in the Records of Littleness' *was first published in the* London Review of Books *on* 11 December 1997. *The* London Review of Books *may be ordered through your local newsagent or taken on subscription. For subscriptions please call on* 0171 209 1141 *or Fax* 0171 209 1151